JULIUS CAESAR

RACHEL FIRTH

ILLUSTRATED BY STEPHEN PARKHOUSE

HISTORY CONSULTANT: DR. ANNE MILLARD
READING CONSULTANT: ALISON KELLY, ROEHAMPTON UNIVERSITY

Edited by Jane Chisholm
Designed by Andrea Slane

First published in 2007 by
Usborne Publishing Ltd.,
Usborne House, 83-85 Saffron Hill,
London EC1N 8RT, England.
www.usborne.com

Printed in China. UE.
First published in America in 2007.

CONTENTS

Chapter 1

Gaius Julius Caesar

It was early morning, and Rome was just beginning to wake up. Tradesmen were opening up their shops, and the delicious smell of freshly baked bread was wafting out of the bakeries. It was going to be a blisteringly hot day.

As Caesar looked down from his balcony, he felt happy to be in the most important city in the world – the heart of the mighty Roman Republic. Anyone who wanted to be anyone came to Rome – and here he was living right in the middle of it. Although he was only 14, he was sure that one day he would have a very important part to play in this great city.

"Gaius, come in and have your breakfast. It's nearly time for lessons." Woken from his daydreams, Caesar reluctantly went inside.

He lived with his mother, Aurelia, his father, Gaius, and his two sisters in a modest house, not far from the forum – a kind of open-air shopping mall. This was the busiest part of Rome.

His family wasn't particularly rich, but it was noble. And there were stories that they were descended from a hero of the ancient city of

Troy, and Venus, the Roman goddess of love, as well as from the ancient kings of Rome.

It was all such a very long time ago. But Caesar was glad that he came from such an important family.

Like other boys of his background, Caesar had a tutor who taught him mathematics, history, philosophy and music. His parents wanted him to become the High Priest of the god Jupiter when he grew up. But Caesar had other ideas.

He wanted to be powerful and famous, and the best way to achieve that was to be a politician. To be a politician, he would have to be really good at oratory – public speaking – and that was the subject he liked best.

When Caesar was 15, his father died, and his life suddenly changed. One of the first things he did was to break off his engagement to a girl, named Cossutia.

Cossutia was rich, but dull. But more importantly, a much better choice of bride had come along.

Caesar's new fiancée was a girl named Cornelia. She came from a highly respected Roman family and she just happened to be the daughter of one of the most powerful men in Rome. She was young, beautiful and graceful, and she had a very large dowry, which would all become Caesar's when they married. The couple decided to get married as soon as possible.

Tragically, Cornelia's father was killed not long after. But this didn't stop Caesar's career from going from strength to strength. He still had powerful connections, and they turned out to be just as useful as he had hoped they would be. Caesar became an officer in the army and was given a junior position in the government.

But then disaster struck. General Sulla seized control of Rome.

Sulla was a brilliant military commander, but a ruthless man and no friend of Caesar's. Caesar's uncle, Marius, had been Sulla's bitter enemy. And, to make things even worse, so had Cornelia's father.

Sulla immediately set about having all his enemies killed, causing a wave of terror throughout the city. He even pinned up a list in the forum of everyone he intended to kill.

One night, Caesar was summoned to his villa. Sulla came straight to the point.

"Julius Caesar," he declared, "you are by rights my enemy. After all, you married the daughter of one of my greatest enemies. But I am prepared to let you live..." Sulla smiled

graciously, "on one condition. Prove your loyalty to me by divorcing Cornelia and marrying someone I choose."

Caesar was stunned. "B-but... I can't... I won't..." he began.

"So be it," Sulla replied, suddenly losing interest. Caesar didn't need to wait until morning to see his name appear on the list. It was time to get out of Rome – fast.

Leaving Cornelia with
his mother, he fled the city right away.
He moved from place to place each night, and
kept on going even when he became sick with
a fever. Finally, one evening, he received a
message from his mother. It was good news.
He had been pardoned.

CHAPTER II

ADVENTURES WITH PIRATES

Caesar returned briefly to Rome. But he wasn't quite ready to stay there just yet, not even to be with Cornelia. He simply didn't trust Sulla. So, instead, he took up a position with the Roman governor of Asia. Soon, he had his first taste of war.

Caesar was sent with a fleet of ships to the Greek island of Mytilene, where the Roman navy had trapped an army of rebels. The rebels were surrounded, but the island was well fortified. There were only two things the Romans could do – starve them out or attack. They decided to attack.

The rebels were soon overwhelmed by the Roman forces, and the battle was over quickly. Too quickly as far as Caesar was concerned – he'd hardly had a chance to fight.

But he had, at least, saved a soldier's life. A rebel was about to run a man through with his sword, when Caesar stopped him in his tracks with a vicious stab to the stomach. He was later awarded an oak wreath for his bravery – one of the most distinguished awards a Roman soldier could receive.

When the last of the rebels had been captured, Caesar set sail for southern Turkey, to serve under the governor there. But it wasn't long before he received some welcome news. Sulla was dead. At last he could return to Rome.

Back home, Caesar was determined to build up his political career. For the next two years, he worked as a lawyer. He didn't always win his cases, but people liked his style. Before long, he gained a reputation as an outstanding speaker.

But even that wasn't good enough for him. He knew he could be even better. So, he sailed to the island of Rhodes, to study with Apollonius Molon, the most famous orator in the world.

Caesar's ship had almost reached Rhodes when it was captured by pirates. They took him to the island of Pharmacussa and demanded a ransom of twenty gold talents. Caesar wasn't intimidated.

"Twenty talents! I'm worth fifty!" he snorted. Clearly, they didn't know how important he was.

"Well, you'd better be worth at least twenty," laughed the pirate chief. "If the ransom's not

Here, fetch me a drink. And don't be so noisy about it. I want some peace and quiet.

paid in six weeks, you'll be dead."

"You'll be paid," replied Caesar, with a sneer, "and when you let me go, I'll come back and kill you all."

For 38 days, Caesar was held prisoner, while his men went off to raise the ransom money. While he waited, he treated his guards more like servants than captors.

But the pirates didn't take his threats at all seriously. It was their biggest mistake.

Just over a month later, the ransom money arrived and Caesar was released. The first thing he did was to hire a fleet and return to the island. He captured the pirates, took their stolen goods for himself and had them all executed – just as he had promised.

Caesar arrived back in Rome a celebrity, but soon after his return, tragedy struck. Cornelia died and Caesar was heartbroken. He gave her the most lavish and expensive funeral possible.

Caesar was now 30, and it was time to take the next step in his career. He applied for a government position, hoping for an important job in the treasury. But instead he was made assistant to the governor of Spain.

Caesar wasn't pleased. He needed to be in Rome if he was to get ahead, but he didn't have much choice. So he consoled himself with the thought that, when his stint in Spain was over, he could come back and join the Senate, Rome's government. Then he'd be at the very heart of Roman politics.

So, as he packed his bags, he resolved to make the best of things, and spend his time in Spain making useful friends and new contacts.

CHAPTER III

A RISING STAR

Ayear later, Caesar was back in Rome and rapidly running out of money. Being a politician was an incredibly expensive business. What with all the bribes and lavish entertaining, not to mention the impressive houses and rich clothes he needed, he owed millions.

Caesar was in big trouble – if he didn't come up with some money quickly, his career would be over.

So he decided to marry a wealthy woman named Pompeia. He didn't love her, but her dowry would be useful – although not enough to get him out of debt. What Caesar needed were friends in high places. There was one man he knew could help him: Senator Marcus Licinius Crassus.

Crassus was one of the richest, most powerful men in Rome. He also happened to like Caesar and agreed to help him out.

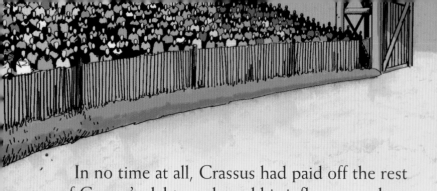

In no time at all, Crassus had paid off the rest of Caesar's debts and used his influence and money to get him the government post of *Curule Aedile*. This meant that he was responsible for public buildings. But, more importantly, it put him in charge of public entertainment. It was the perfect way to win over the people.

Caesar immediately began organizing spectacular festivals and gladiator games.

They cost a fortune, but it was worth it. Anyway, Crassus was paying.

Soon Caesar was the most popular man in town. But he still didn't have any real power. Finally, his chance came. The job of *Pontifex Maximus* – the chief priest of Rome – was up for grabs. Chief priests had a lot of political power and Caesar desperately wanted the position. But first he would have to impress enough senators (government ministers) to vote for him, and competition was stiff.

When the day of the election came, Caesar was very nervous. He'd borrowed a huge

amount of Crassus's money to bribe people to vote for him. If he didn't win, he would never be able to pay him back: he would simply have to flee the country.

Before the vote was cast, each candidate had to make a speech, explaining why he was the best man for the job. After a tense hour, the result was announced. Either Caesar's speech or his bribes had done the trick – or both. He was voted the new chief priest. Now he really was on his way to power and fortune.

Over the next few years, Caesar's career went from strength to strength. He became governor of Spain, led an army against bandits who were terrorizing the country, and somehow managed to make money in the process.

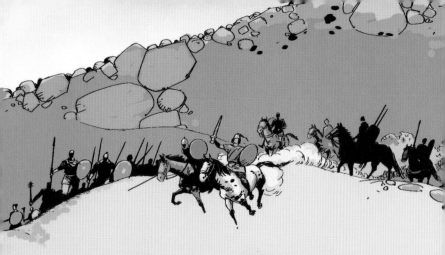

In fact, he made so much that he could afford to pay off his debts, send some money back to the Roman treasury, pay his soldiers well *and* make a substantial profit. The Senate was so impressed, they voted for him to have a triumph.

A triumph was the highest award a commander could have. Celebrations were held all over Rome, with a parade down the main streets. Caesar really wanted a triumph, but he was even more desperate to be a consul. Two people held this position jointly each year, and it was the top job in the Roman government.

But there was a problem. According to the law, a commander wasn't allowed to enter the city to receive his triumph until after the celebrations had begun.

But anyone wanting to be consul had to apply in person a month before the elections. That meant Caesar would have to go to Rome before his triumph started and lose the triumph. If he waited, he would miss the chance to be consul. It was a difficult decision.

Caesar decided to give up the triumph. After all, there were bound to be plenty of other opportunities to win one. Instead, he applied to be consul, and won the election easily. He was now one of the most powerful men in Rome. But he still wanted more, and for that he needed an equally powerful ally. Caesar knew exactly who it should be: Pompey.

Pompey was the most famous general in Rome. He had won victory after victory, and defeated the pirate king, Mithridates. In just five years, Pompey had conquered a total of 1,538 towns and founded 39 new ones.

But his success was starting to worry people. Pompey was becoming too powerful. Many senators feared he might try to take over the Republic. And, with 40,000 fiercely loyal soldiers behind him, he was bound to succeed. He was exactly the type of man Caesar needed on his side. With Crassus's wealth and Pompey's power, there would be no stopping them.

One evening, Caesar invited Pompey and Crassus over for dinner and suggested that the three of them join forces. Crassus wasn't sure at first. He found Pompey arrogant – but Caesar could be very persuasive.

"It's simple," Caesar explained, "you both have money and influence, and I, as consul, have the power to do things. If you support me, I can change a few laws to make life easier for you. Together, we'll be invincible."

Finally, it was all agreed. To seal the deal, Caesar arranged for Pompey to marry his only daughter, Julia.

CHAPTER IV

GLORY ABROAD

After a year, Caesar's term as consul came to an end. It had been a great success. But he was desperately short of money again. He'd spent everything on his grand lifestyle, including thousands on bribes.

As an ex-consul though, he was entitled to become a governor in one or more of the Roman provinces outside Italy. If he picked the right provinces, he would be able to make another fortune and demonstrate his skills as a

brilliant military leader at the same time. He took charge of two provinces in Gaul and one in Illyricum.

But that wasn't enough for Caesar. He recruited an army of 50,000 men, and prepared to invade a part of Gaul which wasn't yet under Rome's control.

For the next two years, he fought the local tribes in Gaul until he had defeated them all. Every time he won a battle, he wrote a gripping account of it and made sure that the news got back to Rome. Each victory meant plenty of cash too, as he demanded huge sums of money from the defeated tribal chiefs.

But his ambitions didn't end in Gaul. Next, he decided to take his army across the Rhine river into Germany, where no Roman general had gone before.

The Germans had already heard what Caesar had done in Gaul, and many of them were so terrified, they surrendered without a fight. Others fled their villages to join allies and wait for Caesar's attack. But he didn't attack.

After stocking up on the corn they had left behind, and burning everything else, Caesar just left.

IRELAND

BRITAIN

Rhine river

English Channel

GAUL

ROMAN OCCUPIED GAUL

CORS

SPAIN

The shaded parts on this map show the places controlled by Rome around the time when Caesar attacked Gaul, Germany and Britain.

Following the tribes into the dense forests in the heart of Germany would be too dangerous, he decided. Besides, he didn't need to do any more.

Most of the Germans near the Rhine had been crushed, and wouldn't be any trouble for some time to come. He'd won fame back home simply by crossing the Rhine, but he wasn't ready to return to Rome just yet. He still had Britain to deal with.

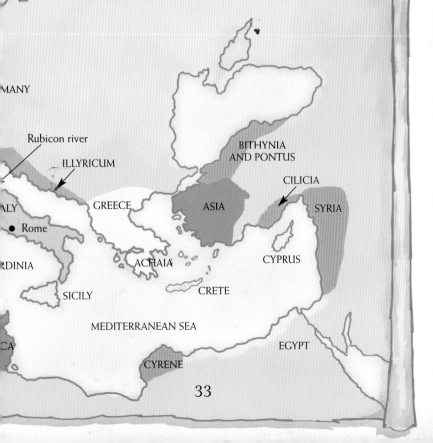

MANY

Rubicon river

ILLYRICUM

BITHYNIA AND PONTUS

CILICIA

GREECE

ASIA

SYRIA

ALY

● Rome

CYPRUS

RDINIA

ACHAIA

CRETE

SICILY

MEDITERRANEAN SEA

EGYPT

CA

CYRENE

The Britons had been helping the Gauls resist the Romans, and Caesar wanted to teach them a lesson. Few Romans had ever set foot in Britain, but that didn't worry him. He marched his army to the coast, and led a fleet of ships across the English Channel.

But the Britons had been warned of the invasion, and they were armed, ready and waiting. When Caesar's men arrived, they were soon met by a force of ferocious British warriors, bearing down on them in chariots and splitting up their ranks.

At first the Britons' tactics caused confusion among the Roman troops, but they soon rallied round, and drove the Britons back. Even so, it wasn't the immediate and overwhelming victory Caesar had hoped for.

So, things weren't going as smoothly as Caesar had expected. He'd thought that the Britons would be so terrified – just at the sight of the Roman army – that they would surrender immediately. He certainly wasn't prepared for fierce resistance. After only 18 days, he decided to leave. He hadn't achieved much, except the glory of being the first Roman general ever to invade Britain. Even so, back in Rome, Caesar was a hero again.

About a year later, Caesar decided to try again. This time, he defeated the British tribes, but he knew they would rebel again, as soon as his back was turned. It would take a lot of effort and money to keep them under control – and it simply wasn't worth it.

So Caesar went back to Gaul, content that the people of Rome would be impressed and thrilled by his latest victory.

But there was bad news waiting for him. His daughter Julia had died giving birth. Caesar was devastated, but he was worried too. As Pompey's wife, Julia had bound Pompey to Caesar. Without her, would Pompey remain his ally?

CHAPTER V

CROSSING THE RUBICON

While Caesar was away, a group of senators were busy stirring up trouble for him back in Rome.

"Who does he think he is?" they said to Pompey. "He has too much power for his own good. Or, more to the point, Pompey, too much power for *your* own good."

"Everyone knows I'm the greatest general Rome has ever had," Pompey replied.

But people could tell he was getting jealous.

Meanwhile, as two groups competed for power in Rome, the ordinary people were becoming restless. There were riots, and they even burned down the Senate House, the government's headquarters. The senators could only think of one solution. They elected Pompey as sole consul and gave him emergency powers to restore order.

By now, Pompey was so jealous of Caesar that he turned against him. He gave the order for Caesar, who was still in Gaul, to disband his army and return to Rome alone – or be declared a traitor. Caesar was furious. Pompey had put him in an impossible situation.

If he went back alone, Pompey would have him executed the moment he walked through the gates. But if he brought his army, Pompey would see it as a declaration of war. There was no alternative: war it would have to be.

With 8,000 soldiers, Caesar set off on the long journey to Rome.

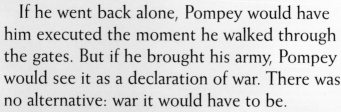

After ten days, they reached the Rubicon, a river marking the boundary between Gaul and Italy. If they crossed it, Caesar knew he would at once be branded a traitor back home. He halted his men so they could rest. Then, he turned to face them.

"It's not too late to stop," he cried, "but if we cross the Rubicon, there will be no going back."

Then Caesar jumped on his horse and rode across the river. His men followed. War had begun.

As they marched on, more and more soldiers flocked to join them, and people came out in droves to cheer them on. Terrified by what was happening, Pompey and some of the senators fled to Greece.

When Caesar and his army finally arrived in Rome, no one tried to stop them from entering the city. And when he declared himself supreme dictator of Rome for a year, some people didn't like it, but few protested out loud. Rome was finally in Caesar's power.

Three months later, he had taken complete control of Italy and defeated some of Pompey's forces in Spain. It was time for a final showdown. He realized Pompey wasn't going to come back to Rome to fight, so he decided to go after him. Leading 20,600 soldiers down to the coast, he and his men set sail for Greece.

Meanwhile, Pompey was marching his army of 42,000 men east, away from Caesar. But Caesar

was hot on his heels. The two armies came face to face at a place called Pharsalus. Caesar had sent for reinforcements, but they hadn't arrived. It was going to be tough beating Pompey's huge army. But there wasn't time to wait. All he could do was attack.

Caesar may not have had as many men, but he was a highly skilled commander. The battle was soon over, and Caesar won.

As soon as Pompey saw that things were going badly for him, he fled to Alexandria, in Egypt, with Caesar in pursuit. The advisers of the young Egyptian ruler, Ptolemy, were afraid of Caesar. Hoping to please him, they had Pompey killed. When Caesar arrived in Alexandria, he was presented with Pompey's ring and his severed head. Caesar was now the sole leader of the Roman world.

CHAPTER VI

CLEOPATRA

Caesar had never wanted to kill Pompey. He had genuinely liked the man. But life was certainly easier now he was dead. It wasn't all plain sailing, though. He still had plenty to do. For a start, he badly needed to pay his army. Luckily, the Egyptians owed the Romans money, so Caesar declared he wasn't going anywhere until they had paid him. He made himself comfortable in an apartment in the royal palace.

Egypt was on the verge of civil war. The country was ruled jointly by Ptolemy and his sister, Cleopatra. But the pair detested one another. Caesar decided to arrange a meeting to try to settle their differences.

The evening before the meeting, there was a knock at his door. A slave ushered in a young Egyptian carrying a rolled-up blanket under his arm. The man lowered his bundle, and announced, "Delivery!"

To Caesar's amazement, a beautiful young woman tumbled out of the blanket.

"Ptolemy isn't fit to run Egypt," Cleopatra declared. "He's only 14 and he doesn't even speak Egyptian – and he's completely under the thumb of that treacherous Greek, Pothinus. I should be the one to rule our country."

Caesar was impressed. Cleopatra was not only beautiful, but proud, intelligent and full of determination. He would help her.

After all, her brother
had been responsible for
Pompey's death. It would do
Caesar no harm in Rome to side
against Pompey's murderer. Besides,
Cleopatra was absolutely captivating.

The next day, Ptolemy arrived early for the meeting and was astonished to find Cleopatra already there. As it dawned on him what had happened, he became absolutely furious and stormed out of the palace.

"This won't be the end of the matter," he snarled.

Ptolemy was right. His scheming adviser, Pothinus, had secretly sent for the Egyptian army. Soon there were 20,000 soldiers marching on Alexandria. Caesar was in big trouble. His own army was a fraction of the size. Before long, Ptolemy had control of most of the city, and Caesar was trapped in the palace.

The palace was well-protected, so the Egyptians couldn't break into it, but they were happy to wait. Caesar's food supplies wouldn't last forever, but Roman reinforcements were on their way. If he could only hold out long enough...

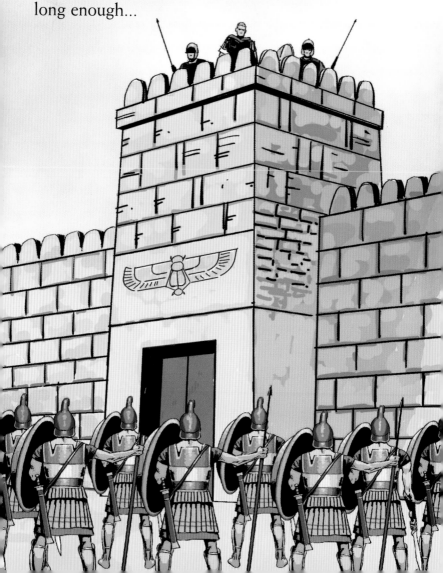

A few months later, thousands of Roman soldiers poured into Egypt. After fierce and bloody battles, Ptolemy was finally defeated. He tried to make his escape by swimming out to a ship heading down the Nile, but he drowned before he could reach safety. Now Cleopatra was in control, and Caesar knew he could rely on her to keep Egypt loyal to Rome.

After a few blissful weeks cruising down the Nile with Cleopatra, it was time for Caesar to leave.

CHAPTER VII

DICTATOR OF ROME

When Caesar finally got back to Rome, the Senate awarded him four triumphs. Caesar decided to celebrate in style, holding them all in the same month. They were to be the greatest victory celebrations ever seen.

There were parades, with dozens of elephants, plays, gladiator contests, chariot races – even a mock naval battle.

Captured kings and warlords were paraded down the streets in chains, and everyone gorged on sumptuous feasts. Meanwhile, the Senate was falling over itself to flatter Caesar and give him more power. At the age of 55, Caesar had achieved almost all his ambitions.

After the excitement of the triumphs had died down, he set about the business of ruling Rome. First, he rewarded his men's loyalty with generous sums of money and land, and offered the very poorest people the chance to start new lives in the provinces, such as Spain and Gaul.

Then, he ordered new buildings to be constructed, including a new forum, named after him. He passed dozens of new laws to try to reduce unemployment, and allowed people from conquered territories to become Roman citizens. He even changed the calendar, which was hopelessly out of step with the seasons.

But some people still weren't happy. However much good he did, Caesar was just too powerful. It was bad enough when the Senate extended his one-year stint as dictator to ten years, but soon after the senators increased his power even more. They voted to allow him to sit with the consuls in the Senate, and have the right to speak first.

Most important of all, they made him dictator for life. This had never happened before, and some of the senators were beginning to be concerned about what Caesar would do next.

Their fears seemed to be confirmed about a year later, on the day of the festival of Lupercalia. It was traditional for young men to run around the city, dressed in animal skins and carrying branches. If a young woman was touched by a branch, it was supposed to bring her good luck.

Caesar was sitting on a throne, dressed in royal purple, watching the festivities. His close friend and ally, Mark Antony, was taking part, so he watched with more interest than usual. There were whoops and cries as women held out their hands hoping to be struck by a branch.

As Antony ran toward Caesar, he seemed absent-mindedly to be twisting a sprig of bay leaves to make what looked like a crown.

Suddenly, he tried to put the crown on Caesar's head. Some people shouted out in approval, but Caesar shrank back. Everyone cheered. Antony tried again, and again Caesar refused. This time, the crowd positively roared.

Senators Cassius and Brutus looked on anxiously. They were more convinced than ever that Caesar was planning to be king.

"Someone has to stop him," they muttered.

CHAPTER VIII

THE FINAL BETRAYAL

A month later, Caesar was strolling toward the temple of Jupiter when he noticed a scruffy old man pushing his way through the crowds. It was Spurinna, a crazy old fortune teller.

"What do you want, Spurinna? Can't you see I'm in a hurry," Caesar snapped.

"Take care, Caesar," Spurinna replied, "especially on the Ides of March. You are in great danger."

Caesar brushed Spurinna aside and increased his pace, but he did feel slightly worried.

On the morning of March 15th (the 'Ides' in the Roman calendar), Caesar awoke early. He was surprised to find his wife out of bed and pacing up and down, her face ashen.

"What is it, my dear?" he asked. "Come back to bed. It's still early. I don't need to leave for the Senate for hours."

"Oh Gaius, you can't go," she sobbed, dropping to her knees. "I had such a terrible dream. You were stabbed to death. It's a warning. Don't go! Oh please, don't go!" she begged.

Caesar smiled at her. "It was just a dream, my love," he said firmly. But he had also had a dream. He dreamed he was flying in the clouds, clasping the hand of Jupiter, the king of the gods. Surely this too was a warning of death?

Caesar took his wife by the hand and drew her to him. "But if you are really worried, I will send a message to the Senate and stay at home today."

An hour later, there was a loud knock on the door and Brutus was shown in.

"Caesar, aren't you coming?"

"There are bad signs today, Brutus," Caesar replied, and explained to him about his wife's dream. "It would be bad luck to hold a Senate meeting."

"Surely you are not going to cancel the meeting because your wife had a silly dream," Brutus frowned. Lowering his voice, he drew Caesar into a corner and whispered, "Look, to be honest with you, the Senate is ready to give you even more power. But, if they don't meet today, who knows what will happen..."

Caesar eventually agreed to go with him. But, as they walked to the Senate, he spotted Spurinna again.

"The Ides have come, Spurinna. And I'm still here!" Caesar shouted cheerfully.

At the Senate, a group of
senators gathered around Caesar,
as they usually did. But he had no idea
that many of them had daggers hidden in
their robes. Suddenly, senator Casca grabbed
Caesar violently by the shoulders, and
stabbed him in the neck. Caesar lashed out,
stabbing Casca's arm with a pen. But it was
no good. As he tried to stand up, he was
struck again. Suddenly, daggers were drawn
on all sides. Caesar was surrounded. There
was nothing he could do. He covered his
head, and sank to the ground as his attackers
stabbed him another 22 times.

Then the conspirators ran off, leaving him
to die in a pool of blood at the foot of a
statue of his former enemy, Pompey.

So ended the life of the man who'd become ruler of the greatest power in the ancient world.

Soon after Caesar's death, Rome was divided by civil war. For 11 years, senators fought it out for control. Finally, Caesar's great-nephew and adopted heir, Octavian, emerged victorious. He became Rome's first emperor – effectively its king. The Roman Republic was gone forever, and the Roman Empire had begun.

My Life

100 BC – I am born.

84 BC – I marry Cornelia.

83 BC – Sulla takes control of Rome and I am forced to flee for my life.

78 BC – Sulla dies and I return to Rome.

76 BC – I am captured by pirates.

69 BC – Cornelia dies.

68 BC – I take up a government position in Spain.

67 BC – I marry Pompeia.

65 BC – I become *Curule Aedile,* which means I am in charge of public entertainment.

63 BC – I am elected *Pontifex Maximus* – Chief Priest of Rome.

62 BC – I divorce Pompeia.

61-60 BC – I am governor of Spain. Crassus, Pompey and I make a secret agreement to support each other politically.

59 BC – I become consul. I also marry Calpurnia, and Pompey marries my daughter, Julia.

58-51 BC – I lead successful campaigns in Gaul.

55 BC – My army crosses the Rhine into Germany and, later in the year, we invade Britain.

54 BC – I invade Britain for the second time. Julia dies.

54 BC – The Senate makes Pompey sole consul.

49 BC – My army and I cross the Rubicon river and civil war in the Republic of Rome begins. I march to Rome and become dictator for one year. Pompey flees to Greece.

48 BC – I defeat Pompey. He flees to Egypt where he is murdered by the Egyptians. I meet Cleopatra and defeat her brother's army.

46 BC – I become dictator for ten years.

45 BC – The last of my enemies are defeated and civil war comes to an end. In February, I become dictator for life.

44 BC – **Caesar was murdered on the Ides of March (March 15th).**